Beautiful Chaos

A FREE VERSE REFLECTION

By
Q.M. Gatlin

Copyright Notice 2024

Disclaimer

This book contains journaling pages; for those who have opted to journey via e-book. It is suggested that you make your notations separately on notebook paper, as the e-book does not give you the option to click and fill in with writing.

Table of Contents

ABOUT THIS BOOK

This book was written as a passion project over the course of years through experiences, learning, living and seeing the through a lens of others experiences from vicarious connection.

This is meant to serve as reflective literature. Sometimes verbalizing one's feelings, thoughts and experiences can be difficult. The poetry and journaling chapters serve as a tool in processing, reflecting and opening up into perspective thinking. Every poem and illustration are abstract and can hold different meanings for different individuals.

I hope that you can dive into these chapters with an open mind and readiness. If this book can help just one person; then it has truly done its job.

DEDICATION

This book is dedicated to those that never felt truly seen, heard or that their voice wasn't big enough…

Reach Out

If you or someone you know is battling with mental health issues, suicidal thoughts or substance abuse please reach out to call or text 988 for 24/7 support. Link below:

https://988lifeline.org/

CHAPTER REFLECTION **1**

FOOD FOR THOUGHT

Faith without work is dead. There are many mentioning's of this quote, said in various ways; whether we find it in religious, spiritual or mantra sayings. The power behind the words remains the same. It is not enough to only wish the will of something. Active investment in the want contributes far into the outcome.

WHAT IS ONE OF YOUR DESIRED GOALS?
Ex. I desire to find balance in my weekly schedule & prioritize.

_____

_____

_____

_____

WHAT CAN YOU ACTIVELY CONTRIBUTE TO MANIFEST YOUR GOAL?

_____

_____

_____

_____

Crashed

The rhythm to which my body drifted
The vibration in which my mind jounced

All so apparent, that the outcome of this is the ending
But at this very moment there is nothing more I can do

Hurdles of waves crash into me
Lines of wind swirl around me one by one

Another then another

Each thump into by body, releasing a flash into my skull

If effervescent bubbles of turmoil were painted as a
moment
It would be a lot like this

My mind fizzled as my heart pounded
Leading my body to still

Sounds were no more as lights began to fade out

Flashes of memories slowed as the thumps of my beating
pulse stopped

It was at that moment I felt the pieces of my soul float
around me

The realization daunting
I was already too late

To see what had become of me
Visual evidence sinking to the bottom floor

Time was up, if only I had tried to fight
Oh, but alas I had already Crashed.

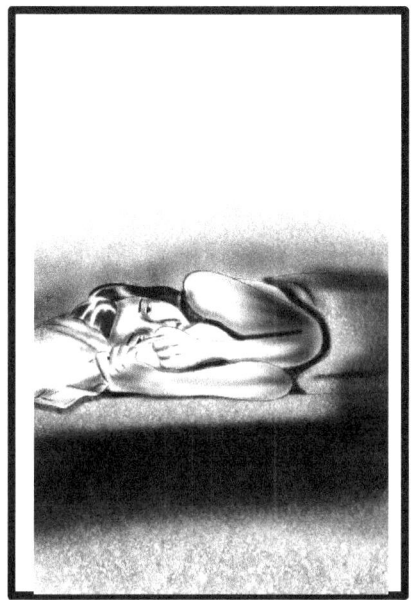

Sleeping Awake

You know it's the funniest thing

I have blinked and awoken

My eyes are partially open

Now my feet are on the ground

This out of body experience feels very peculiar

In this awake state

I continue to DREAM

Melatonin drowsiness

Clouds my view

Chamomile energy

Bounce off my visual sheets

With not a more complex blanket

Then the human mind

My will has caffeinated me

Visions are strong and DREAMS are cemented

With a flashlight for back up

Slippers on the cold floor

Life waits for me

I am no longer in masked slumber

No way to go back

In a covered-up cycle of sleep

Now moving forward, I will be Sleeping Awake.

Embrace

Maybe it was in the way of your touch,
or could it be the way your words caressed the air.

Each syllable spoken,
created a growing thickness in the room.

Causing the fibers to break through my walls,
making any will power to slip inch by inch.

Was it not enough to cause micro trembles,
would you really push me to bare my soul to?

The closer you sauntered into my immediate space,
it unraveled more of the webs of a maze I built.

My inner being began to crumble,
if just maybe for a second you would halt.

Somehow, I fear it is already too late,
making direct eye contact was such an amateur move.

Betrayed by the glint in my eyes,
outed display of raised prickles on my skin.

The inner fight is over,
before it has had the chance to begin.

Only choice I have left,
let your reach consume me; as I welcome the embrace.

CHAPTER REFLECTION **2**

FOOD FOR THOUGHT

Often times as we age throughout adulthood, we find that we get stuck in critical stages of life. These may be areas where trauma is brought to the forefront or simply areas, we lack development in because teachings in these areas were non-existent. It is important in these moments to personify the adult to yourself that you needed as a kid.

WHAT'S A PAST OR UPCOMING MILESTONE IN YOUR LIFE:

_____

_____

_____

_____

ARE THERE WAYS THAT YOU CAN OR COULD HAVE CREATE (ED) AN AIDING SPACE FOR THIS?
Ex. Ask a trusted friend or family member to supply you with words of encouragement or support during a particular milestone. To really aid this space ask this particular trusted person to be present at your milestone.

_____

_____

_____

_____

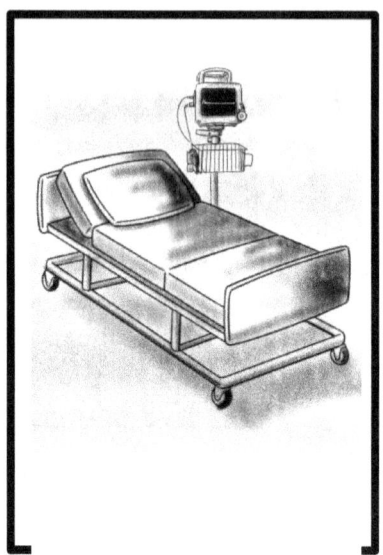

Operation

With the finesse of the sharpest blade

Sweat beads roll over the skin of every masked face

Just a matter of moments

Wrapped into the scene

One cut too deep

One nip too light

Just a matter of moments

Wrapped into the scene

The clock won't let up!

It Tic Toc's so LOUD

Machines being boisterous

There is no turning back now

Just a matter of moments

Wrapped into the scene

The countdown has been given

Cannot turn back now

Suddenly! BEEP _____displayed on the machine

Oh man, what have I done?

This was supposed to be the start of my desired dreams

Time

One of the most precious things experienced in life
Just a little more is what the elders say
Speed things up, I can't wait is what the youth shout
Maybe a bargain or a trade is what mid lifers battle.
Funny or Ironic that time is elusive
With no bounds or cheat sheets
Its fountain of youth limitless
Yet it's lived as an individual lottery

Such a priceless gift is hard to be measured

Is there a meter to set the allotment of its worth

The one thing that can never be returned once it is given

Fleeting every second of the day

Slept away at night in the eons of space

Gone by morning before an open of an eye

Ticking in a cadence

Toking through schedules

No matter the flow that it is used

In partial to the arrangements set up

It is wise to recognize the power and beauty

Of the gift notoriously called Time

Tree Filled

Each one planted,
is a living soul.
Rooted deep, deep into the ground.

It would be nice to live as long as they do,
just to see them continue to grow.

Leaf by leaf,
they fall off into autumns throne.

Beautiful Chaos

It is then we know
That a new season is home.

I often talk,
and they listen.

With no words,
no invalidation of my jumbled thoughts,
no judgement,
no lashing of discomfort.

It's quite nice, you know
to have such non-verbal support.

When the tree's bloom,
Oh, they don't just bloom;
They burst!!

Shades of leaves and flowers,
spilling into the streets like brushstrokes;
painting a grounded portrait.

To think they always save a spot just for me,
under their shade.

No RSVP necessary,
Enough room for a few more,
Each tree has just enough space,

To think.
To breathe.
To just be.

CHAPTER REFLECTION 3

FOOD FOR THOUGHT

Criticism plays a big role in how we see ourselves. The effects of criticism are multidimensional as it relates to one's mind, thoughts and actions. When your younger and you do something good; the adults clap and cheer. This signals to your brain in development repeat these actions.

However, when you do something displeasing you receive the "no-no" talks and the not so cheery faces. Thus, triggering negative feelings toward those actions. The same concept reigns true in adulthood. Not necessarily with an action or thought being right or wrong; however, these very things are criticized by others. Typically, we can be our own toughest critics.

REFLECT ON SOMETHING THAT YOU ARE HARD ON YOURSELF ABOUT? IS THERE ROOM TO GIVE YOURSELF GRACE IN THIS AREA?

_____

_____

_____

_____

Should Be

To the father who refused to bend and the son that could
not mold; the father taught lesson after lesson, while the
son needed those three words sown.

The father only gave what was passed to
him, the son needed the cycle to change;
Hour after hour; Years created blood, sweat and tears.

Somehow it was not enough;

The son only ever needed to hear those words of praise given to him, then he would be glad to battle the world.

Only so close at the tip of the father's tongue,
Yet when he generated the words, no sound would come out.

To become his own man, what a sight that would be,
if only his father could offer a proud form of decree.

The son-maintained hope that if only one day the father would come around to see his inner cry battle of mental struggles and plea.

Maybe just maybe, a tiny wisp of recognition would fill the air. On that day the son and father reach common ground
Placing away the blocks of stumble, in the way it should be.

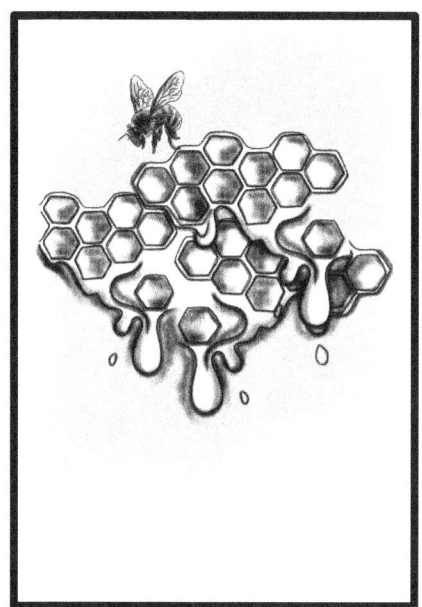

Unfiltered

The bee by the tree

Who buzzed and buzzed with glee

Did more than its part

To give to this world

All the bots did was take, take, take, take

Without a care

How absurd

As the takers filled their projects

Full of the bee's honey

They became depleted

As no one gave back a fraction of its abundance

The Bee who once had glee

Had to retreat from its favorite tree

bots took not once notice

Only felt dismay for the lack of the honey seeds

So now you see

By what was done to the bee

People will take until you break

It's okay to retreat

Sometimes a break from the pressure

Of nonstop is the only way to be free.

Born from Fire

The lights were shining brightly

The sounds became overwhelming

It took time to adjust

Surroundings were new

Slate clear as crystal glass

Sensory soared in vibrance

Smells of newness

With just a touch of memory

Another chance to get it right

Different paths to create

Relearning motion and movement

One foot at a time

The past burned in ashes

Up unscathed and standing

Not a moment to waste

Automatically Scattering old habits

New days await over the horizon

This time rebirth is different

Triggered was the phoenix

What a flame life will be

CHAPTER REFLECTION 4

FOOD FOR THOUGHT

Words have power! One word can be the difference between rebirth and destruction. It is pivotal to speak kind words to ourselves. A great way to practice this would be to make affirmations a practiced habit.

WHAT ARE THREE AFFIRMATIONS YOU WOULD LIKE TO AFFIRM TO YOURSELF DAILY?

_____

_____

_____

_____

_____

_____

_____

_____

_____

_____

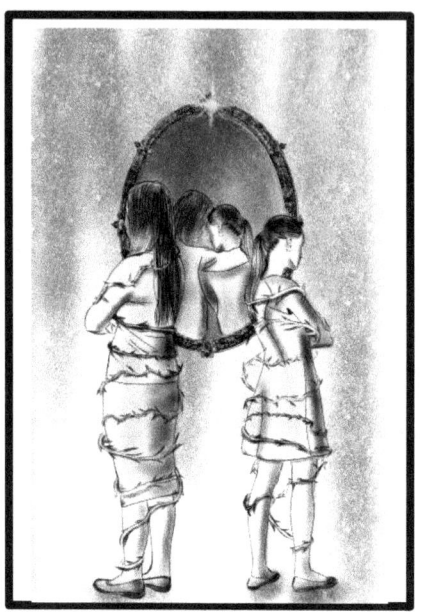

Could Be

To a mother who gave the all of who she was; to the daughter that couldn't understand why there wasn't more.

To the mother who could never read the words;

To the daughter at a young age who could read,

yet couldn't comprehend at first.

To a mother who wanted nothing more than to share her
love, only the how
became a complication.

To the daughter who needed to receive that love, only to
be met with
clouded filtration.

Some say be the adult to the inner child that may have
needed; but what happens when the inner mirror of
your cortex forms defense mechanisms of being
jaded.

The daughter only ever wanting to hug her, to love her
and embrace her the days there was fear. The mother gave
all of who she was, teaching from what she held the
capacity of inside.

If only the two could understand each other, accept what
was given through the years of tears; tear down those
faded colored walls. Form a bond in uncharted territory,
who knows what it could be.

Moon

Penetrating glimmers of light through the darkest shadows

One of the three that can never be hidden

Creating moments of levitational pull

Seen from many gaps and spaces around the world

The changes affecting phases of life

Behaviors with contributing attributes

Reshaping constantly to the human eye

The stars laminate around you

To stare and gaze at you in the night

Is to stare and capture a frame of space

Lighting paths in the darkness

Glowing orbit as a phenomenon

Many around the world have raced to your base floor

Even as they touched you

Never has there been a full containment

To embody all of your grace

Continue to shine and light the way

In balance with the sun

Forever in time

Never to be hidden ancient beauty in the skies

Silently Loud

Surrounded by company all around

How is it I am still alone; when I see them all making sounds

So many faces of joy and smiles with cheer

This is a happy moment for me, but my energy is fleeting low

My third eye shut down and now I'm all choked up

How is the inner voice of doubt loud with crude remarks?

I wonder can they hear them; The doubts speak so loudly!!

This is supposed to be a perfect moment

I must turn this around

As I struggle to move the lines on my face

Placing them at rest

My conscious mind and ego battle it out in a slow-motion pace

The walls try to close, but at the last second, I have found grace

I use my voice to vocalize noise and equalize this silently loud place

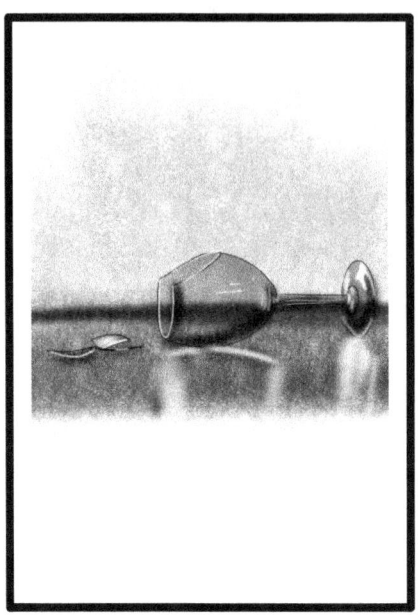

Sobriety

Can't really decipher if it was the thoughts or the need.

Hands shaking and head filled with massive sweat beads.

Thoughts racing and running rapid with my mind spinning around.

If I don't get what I need soon, it's a chance I might drown.

It shouldn't be this hard to get through my day.

What have I started and done to cause my body disarray.

I promised I would stop and I could quit any time.

I still manage to have good days; I am still in my prime.

This time will count and I will quit now for sure.

Fall ten times and get up again, I grabbed the knob to walk

through the chosen sober door.

CHAPTER REFLECTION 5

FOOD FOR THOUGHT

Have you ever stared at a screen so long that your eyes began to get blurry or unfocused? Sometimes all you need is to shut your eyes and get give them a gentle rest; this then resets your vision and once again you are able to see clearly what is on your screen.

It is important that we take rests from certain things in order to give ourselves a reset. This can mean stepping away from social media for a few weeks, declining an event every now and then. The list is endless.

REFLECT ON SOMETHING YOU WOULD LIKE TO RESET ON. THEN WRITE IT DOWN AND GIVE YOUR SELF A REALISTIC TIME FRAME OF REST. MAKE SURE TO LIST WHAT YOU HOPE TO ACCOMPLISH ONCE YOU'VE REACHED YOUR RESET:
Ex. Take one week a month to rest from staying up past 11pm. I hope to gain a more restful state of mind once I reach my reset.

_____

_____

_____

_____

Sun

Lighting up the world

Shining rays on the darkest days

Big contributions to many harvest

Prickle feelings along the skin

Caressing the top of the ocean

Drying the weeping left on the ground

Given images of happiness

Representing joy across the land

Free vitamins you give
Spreading nourishing haze

Working in tandem with your partner
Who supplies lighted darkness and cooling watts
Power so great beyond comprehension
No way to directly peek and look above
Keep burning bright
Lighting the way

Mays new generations of tomorrow
Use your guidance and treat you better
With preservation and education
They can implement if we empower

Not Alone

Today in bed I stayed,
where my mind remained grounded.

Thus, time slowed down,
coincidently my smile stayed reversed at a frown.

I tried moving with little success of motion,
living was placed as the farthest palatable notion.

It's not as though I lack the will,
sometimes completing the day is such a battle rattled hill.

There are some who will never understand,
believing that things take only a positive command.

Some out there do know these experiences to be true,
the ones who've battled some odd days that were the
deepest shades of black and blue.

I can only hope if you are like me,
you will reach out for help when your mind hears only
inner siren pleas.

So many routes and ways to pull forward,
this is validation that you've been heard and it's not over.

However, much fight that is left inside yourself,
find a little bit more and take a leap of faith on
possibilities of life's wealth.

I hope that wherever in the world that you are,
you hold on.

Because to someone, you may be their moon and stars.

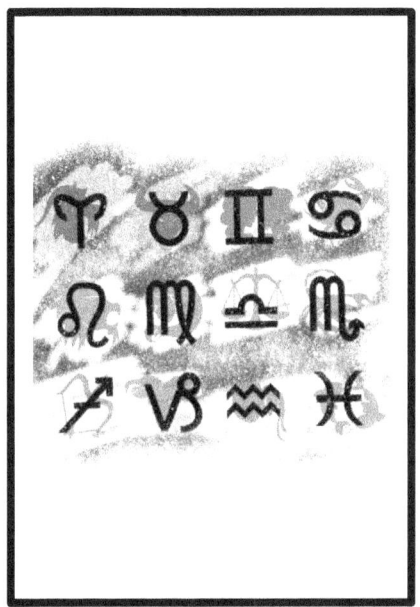

Zodiac Master Class

Aries Took the Lead

Taurus Remained Persistent

Cancer Offered Support

While Scorpio Stayed Driven

Sagittarius Flowed as Versatile

Aquarius Was Inventive

Leo Offered Generosity

To People's Needs Pisces Was Sensitive

Gemini Displayed Balanced Intelligence

Capricorn Words Were Patient

Virgo Practiced Logical Humbleness

Libra Offered Harmonious Intention

CHAPTER REFLECTION **6**

FOOD FOR THOUGHT

Fear can be incapacitating. Fear is a response that can be internal/external which stems from an awareness or anticipation of danger which can be real or imagined. In this chapter reflection pitstop; ponder on any fears you are experiencing that may form a barrier in achieving one of your goals.

LIST A GOAL THAT HAS BEEN STIFILED BY FEAR:
Ex. Applying for a promotion at work

_____

_____

_____

IF YOU KNEW THAT YOU COULD REMOVE ONE OF THOSE FEARS, WHAT WOULD IT BE?
Note: The idea is to mentally remove these barriers so that taking the steps toward fears that will create growth and elevation become within a better reach.

Ex. I would remove denial of a promotion being possible.

_____

_____

_____

Tribe

Not alone, Not Out-casted, No Tables for One.

Building blocks of trust

Deep roots of great stock

Collaborations are ingrained

Teams coming together

Rolodex full with people

Count grows along the path

The journey is meaningful

Enhanced collective sparks

When the road gets bumpy

Turn to see

The many rows are filled

With a Tribe busting through the seams

Action Stroll

Excited and Giddy;
So full of life!

Passion burning through my soul:
Cleansed with rain inside.

Energy of the world;
Moves and flows limitlessly.

Whispers of the ocean scent;
Shining out of sight on the scene.

The finest sand under my feet;
Setting the stage in my mind.

What a joyous momentum;
Action moves up ahead taking the reins on my time!

Fated Mate

I knew right away what you were to me
My heart skipped to many beats past possible

I felt your pressing presence, before I ever saw your face
Your aurora tapped into mine and began to open my
chakras

I knew right then and there what my future held
There was no way to unawake or alert myself now

I saw the silhouette of your deepest dream
You sunk your third eye into mine

I understood at that very moment life would never be the same
With you I could enhance my wholeness beyond measure

You would forever be the glow to my sun
I would in turn forever be the brightness to your moon

We would for the rest of our days light the path forever for each other

As my mate, in tuned soul, you my love, would forever be my HOME.

CHAPTER REFLECTION 7

FOOD FOR THOUGHT

It is often said that there is not enough time in the day. Days hold 24 hours within them. Within that the average person clocks in about roughly 6 hours of sleep. Leaving 18 hours; from this we factor an average 8-hour work shift. This then leaves us 10 hours. Stay with me now... Somewhere in these 10 hours there needs to be room commuting, hygiene, eating, restroom breaks etc. This can cause overwhelming feelings when it comes to time management. While this is not a one size reflects all; it gives a descriptive depiction on time and the need for prioritizing when it can all be overwhelming. Especially if you begin to factor in if applicable family, friends and other commitments that require needed time. Sometimes setting the pace with prioritizing can go a long way.

LIST 5 TOP PRIORITIES:

_____

_____

_____

LIST 5 SECONDARY PRIORITIES?

_____

_____

_____

Gone from Me

So unfair!

This Cannot be True.

How?

Why?

What made you leave me?

You visited my dream last night,

told me it would be okay.

Gave me one last moment of wisdom,

graced me with one last hug.

Who told you that it was okay to LEAVE ME?
What made you think that it was right?
Heaven gained an angel...
But me! I lost part of my
inner shine. Wont you come
back to me, just one last time.
I know that's not how this works,
it's no longer your time.
I promise to make you proud,
Be the best version of me I can be.
Save me a seat among the clouds,
for when we once again meet.

Love

It's that moment of feeling gooey
Butterflies flutter down the spine
Or maybe it was the stomach
Love sure is sublime

It's so patient and understanding
Craved all the time
Supposedly it's unconditional

Unfiltered like corked wine

There is no cap on what is allowed
The rules are very clear
So many variations of love
Warm thoughts when it's near

The heart holds so much
While the brain registers it all
Love is a complex beautiful entity
Just have to be willing to answer the call

Natal Rise

You found me again
I should be thankful
Not really sure if I am ready
Even so this day holds power

Wisdom should be seeping in
From everything I have learned
Wonder if those life lesson will take

Will there be lights or candles that are worn

Many acknowledgments will come
Forgotten minds will not bother
Nothing I can do at this point
It's been written on paper

Casting unfinished annual milestones aside
focusing on the right here and now
More time to accomplish
New moons with new suns
Happy Birthday is in order as I ascend into a new dawn

They and Them

They said I couldn't do it
That it could never be done

Oh, how I trusted them
Now look what I have done

They told me to give up
Give in and just quit

I truly believed them
Now I am stuck with only little grit

They played me like a fiddle
I was their own private joke

Nothing good came from any of them
Now with my pride I must soak

They are the naysayers
So many all around

One thing I have to give to them
They <u>ALMOST </u>knocked off my CROWN

CHAPTER REFLECTION 8

FOOD FOR THOUGHT

In earlier chapter reflections we touched on goals, fear and metaphorically hitting the reset button. In this reflection space we will touch on purging or rather cleansing a space. While cleansing one's mind creates wonderful head space. Cleansing a physical space can be equally euphoric. Letting go of personal stuff can be extremely difficult and for some will cause great duress. However, if you are in a space and ready to make that leap for spatial cleansing; start small and pick one room. If a room is big undertaking, start with a section of one room.

AS YOU LOOK AT THE SPACE YOU'VE SELECTED. ACKOWLEDGE HOW BIG OF A STEP YOU HAVE TAKEN TO GET TO THIS POINT OF CLEANSING YOUR SPACE. NOTATE HOW YOU FEEL BEFORE BEGINNING.

_____

_____

_____

_____

_____

_____

_____

_____

ALL DONE! HOW FAR DID YOU GET IN YOUR CLEANSING? WHAT WAS THE PROCESS LIKE? IS THIS SOMETHING YOU CAN SEE YOURSELF DOING AGAIN?

_____

_____

_____

_____

_____

_____

_____

_____

Too Late

Something just isn't right
I can see it in your stare
I feel it in the atmosphere

The shuddered shift makes me cringe
My palms begin to sweat
Your brows form a line

It could be the something you aren't saying
More like the language of your body yells
There is a thump getting louder

Sounds a lot like my heart
Something makes my glands rise up
Your much closer than I thought

The slight squeak gets more frequent
As you take more steps toward me
Now I realize you've gotten closer
Cornered me in the dark

There was something I wanted to say
Maybe a way to plead my case
I was so sure I was paying attention

Somehow your closer, it's too late
The bulbs break ONE by ONE
Glass shatters everywhere

No need to hold my breath
I have no choice in my frame of fear

A slight movement from my body
Involuntary attempt in retreat
All of a sudden quiet,
eerie then BAMM, I can
no longer FLEE!!!

Dropped to the ground
My air has gone away
You snuffed out my life for good
Took my ability to breathe

So many ambitions
Why did I wait?
It doesn't matter anymore, now it's TOO LATE

Pathways

Seeking clear paths and polished roads,
but at times there was only dirt and gravel.

Wanting to skip ahead 5 steps but instead, I was
buried 10 feet down without so much as a shovel.

Tried to keep my supply box new, fresh and neat,
however; could never find the exact tool I needed.

As I grew older, I thought I would surely have the all of
the answers. But curve balls showed me some
problems will seek, sow and become deep weeded.

The perfect circle that I envisioned was on my board.
Unknowingly, some of my circle would only be there
for a season.

Picket fence and maybe 2.5 kids;
plans change, pending dates and alter for good reason.

There was a career I planned for many years in
advance, but paths change all the time.

Directives on where I should be, started plaguing my
mind.
The older I become; I suppose the wiser I should be.
The one thing I learned is to live in certain moments and
let some things reign free.

This doesn't mean stop pushing for goals, plans or
even dreams.
But it does speak to enjoying the journey; the destination
is our legacies marquee.

Travel

To see all the places
So much different than mine
To pack up my suitcase
Choosing between driving or flying

So much to see
Even more to go and explore
Dreams of visiting the corners of the world
Gliding the clouds as we soar

A tchotchke here
A magnet from over the there

Trading money for accurate currency
The many outfits I get to wear

Trying to decide if I should take a picture
Maybe film a video to later see
Deliberations to live in the moment
Being present just might be the key

I won't take it for granted
Traveling I mean
So many have never seen the ocean
Gratitude in movements that are free

Piece of Me

Fragments at their core are incomplete
Pieces in life that are disconnected
Apart from life's main clause

Together each part of a fragment holds life
All on their own the life would not be complete

As each day begins again
Chances to reevaluate our formation as a person
Ways to determine and mold a different outcome

No matter the mistakes
No matter the regrets

However big the dreams
Each fragments contributes pieces
That weave and form to our life vignettes

Darkness

Here I am invisible

So stranded and alone

Will people realize I am missing?

Even when we are in the same room

There is nothing but despair

Feelings of duress

If only I would just say something

Maybe then through this dark cloud

Someone, anyone could see or hear me

Tomorrow is a new day
But first I must survive this
The walls keep closing in
I battle with the will to not give in
It's so hard when this happens
It can't be framed into words
If a little of this darkness
Would start to subside
I could pick myself up again
And live tomorrow anew
Putting steps into drive
No longer swallowed by complete darkness
All I need is a little of the moon to shine

CHAPTER REFLECTION 9

FOOD FOR THOUGHT

REALATIONSHIPS Are a catalyst in the development in our life story. The best relationship can uplift the fabric of who we are; while the worst relationships can pull the thread out of the embodiment of who we are. All relationships have an invisible time stamp on them. Relationships can be formed for a Reason, Season or a Lifetime. It is important to understand the bases of each relationship held so that the accurate energy can be given. Every type of relationship will feel and look different. For an example a relationship dynamic will be different with a mentor vs a sibling, spouse or work friend.

REFLECT ON WHAT RELATIONSHIPS MEAN TO YOU AND WHAT YOU SEEK FROM EACH TYPE OF RELATIONSHIP. THIS WILL GIVE YOU A TOOL TO NAVIGATE AN UNDERSTANDING THE DYNAMICS OF YOUR RELATIONSHIPS BETTER. IT IS ALSO A GOOD IDEA TO REFLECT ON WHAT YOU ATTRIBUTE TO EACH OF THESE RELATIONSHIPS:

_____

_____

_____

_____

It's You, Not me

How dare you try to trick me?
Did you think I would be blinded by your lies?

I must say you're a fast one
Every time I add you up
You seem to keep on the rise

Any time I take away just a little from you
You begin to act oh so dramatic with your display of
negative loss

Somehow the sneaky opportunist in you
Squirms and sneaks out

Anytime there's more than one option
Your operation multiplies about

Not very faithful
With your forever divided time
Even when you run out of positive numbers
You still continue your crimes

So, you see it's you and not me
You've done this to us way too much
I think I will stick to other subjects
Ones that don't give my brain such unjust

Math, my dear we are over
Let's see other people, oh please
Well at least until rent is due

Then I will need to borrow your expertise

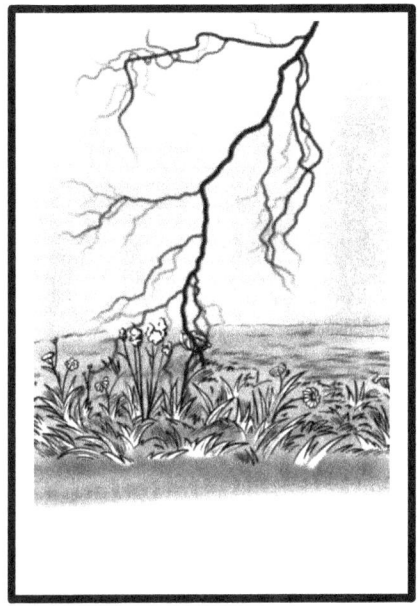

Energy

Such a delicate gem energy is
It can't be remade or destroyed

Transferred from one entity to the next
Must protect it and use it wisely

For it is the cusp of reality
Where sanity battles chaos in war

The Audacity That Is Me

How dare I tell you to throw that
away, how dare I make you choose.

What was once an object close to your
heart, I threw it out of my view.

Out of my peripheral, out of your
space. Out of my sight,
why couldn't I just STOP and SEE?

Why couldn't l look closer to the objects that you once
held dear.

To the objects that held comfort during times that weren't always serene.

I knew you needed extra care with your mind from the day to day.

Yet and still; being one tracked minded I by passed the choice away.

I see NOW I see CLEAR,
It was never my choice to choose.

My job was to support you,
even if my understanding is a ruse.

What matters most is that you're okay,
that you are now able to get through your day.

Whether you need the transitional object in a collection, or even just one.

The next time I will come to you, I will listen…
because the choice of the matter was always your right to choose.

Q.M Gatlin

Out of Body Out of Mind

Who is this person that I am seeing
The one staring back at me

Feels like an imposter
Only their features match me

I don't like this feeling
The emotions I feel inside

One minute I am okay for a bit
Then the next I explode like a Tide!

Oh great! Now people are looking at me
All they do is judge and stare

Having not one form of a clue what it's like
To change in moments and not being prepared

My brain hasn't been working right
Lately it's a bit off

Doctors give more test and medicine
Friends and family write me off

They say I'm not the same
Well thanks for stating the obvious captain
Would you like a cookie or a star?

It's all a big joke
People sure do get their laughs
Or, wait is it pity?
I don't know my filters are off from the crash

Life will never be the same it seems
I wish I could understand
If only the familiar stranger staring back at me could feel
me in or reel me back from this trance staring at me

CHAPTER REFLECTION **10**

FOOD FOR THOUGHT

Sometimes we may have so much in our bucket of life that it feels like it's ready to tip over. What tips over one person's bucket may not be the same for the next person. It is important to understand what sustains your well-being. Having self-care as a possible source can do wonders for mental health. If you find that you don't know where to start with balancing out. It may be imperative to then seek assistance with guiding your life towards equilibrium.

REFLECT ON WHO YOU CAN REACH OUT TO IF YOUR BUCKET FEELS LIKE IT MAY TIP OVER:

_____

_____

_____

_____

WHAT ARE WAYS YOU CAN ATTRIBUTE SELF CARE INTO YOUR LIFE? IS YOUR CHOICES OF SELFCARE SUSTAINABLE?

_____

_____

_____

_____

Webbed Creation in Hand

What is the feeling from this creation I have made
Living breathing and so full of life

In stunned in amazement at this wonderful sight
So many weaves and paths of a web they may take

Only in the palm of my hands for 1/10th of a shake
Before I know it, you will grow right before my eyes

Let me bask in this moment, as my tears start to dry
These are tears of joy, maybe confusion and fear

I know one thing is certain, I would give you my last
and only air

We may not always get it right all of the time

By your side and at your six , is where I will hover in
line; your lines forever connected to me and many
more far back on a weaved growing tree

Love so unconditional, so many stored legacy items you
shall have

I stare at your features to memorize the smell

The memory connected to more feelings
that dwell

Any thoughts of you and my heart will forever swell

Broken Clock

Tell me this, is it true?
I have myself to blame

It was always tomorrow, tomorrow, tomorrow
Only I kept pushing it back yet another day

So many things I wanted to accomplish, many things I
thought I'd get to share

It was always a reason I gave myself on why my time I
couldn't spare

It wouldn't be fun
You may not like it
That just seems a bit too far

Now look at the moment present
The space to create a new memory is but a farse

Now I must forgive myself
Activate loving grace
Really as in realistically
It's a cop-out not to feel the squeeze in my heart

Days come and they go
Life zooms by so fast
It has no age limit to its cut off

To wishes of better plans
We can't go back in time

Just one more argument I'd spare
Take you to the store you liked

But all we have now, is a snuffed out broken clock

Bonus Reflections

Ready to take the 15 Day Challenge ?

Turn the page and let's get started!

Note: Morning prompts remain the same to challenge follow thru and self-accountability. <u>Evening prompts differ each day during the challenge.</u>

DAY 1

CHAPTER REFLECTION BONUS

FOOD FOR THOUGHT

15 Day Challenge Journal Reflection Tracking

MORNING:

WRITE DOWN 2 OR 3 AFFIRMATIONS TO START THE DAY:

_____

_____

_____

_____

WHAT IS YOUR TOP 3 PRIORITIES FOR TODAY?

_____

_____

_____

_____

EVENING:

WHAT IS ONE CHALLENGE THAT YOU EXPERIENCED THIS WEEK?

_____

_____

_____

_____

HOW DID YOU OVERCOME OR MANAGE THE LISTED CHALLENGE?

_____

_____

_____

_____

DAY 2

CHAPTER REFLECTION BONUS

FOOD FOR THOUGHT

15 Day Challenge Journal Reflection Tracking

MORNING:
WRITE DOWN 2 OR 3 AFFIRMATIONS TO START THE DAY:

_____

_____

_____

_____

WHAT IS YOUR TOP 3 PRIORITIES FOR TODAY?

_____

_____

_____

_____

EVENING:

WRITE DOWN AT LEAST ONE SHORT TERM GOAL THAT YOU WANT TO ACCOMPLISH AT THE END OF THIS 15 DAY CHALLENGE:

_____

_____

_____

_____

LIST ACTIONS/STEPS NEEDED TO ATTAIN THIS GOAL(S):

_____

_____

_____

_____

DAY 3

CHAPTER REFLECTION BONUS

FOOD FOR THOUGHT

15 Day Challenge Journal Reflection Tracking

MORNING:

WRITE DOWN 2 OR 3 AFFIRMATIONS TO START THE DAY:

_____

_____

_____

_____

WHAT IS YOUR TOP 3 PRIORITIES FOR TODAY?

_____

_____

_____

_____

EVENING:

WHAT IS ONE THING YOU WANT TO SAY TO YOUNGER YOU?

_____

_____

_____

_____

LIST ANY ADMIRATIONS YOU HAVE FOR YOUNGER YOU:

_____

_____

_____

_____

DAY 4

CHAPTER REFLECTION BONUS

FOOD FOR THOUGHT

15 Day Challenge Journal Reflection Tracking

MORNING:

WRITE DOWN 2 OR 3 AFFIRMATIONS TO START THE DAY:

_____

_____

_____

_____

WHAT IS YOUR TOP 3 PRIORITIES FOR TODAY?

_____

_____

_____

_____

EVENING:

WHICH PRIORITY DID YOU ACCOMPLISH?

_____

_____

_____

_____

WHAT STOPPED YOU IF ANYTHING FROM COMPLETING ALL 3 PRIORITIES FROM THE MORNING PROMPT?

_____

_____

_____

_____

DAY 5

CHAPTER REFLECTION BONUS

FOOD FOR THOUGHT

15 Day Challenge Journal Reflection Tracking

MORNING:

WRITE DOWN 2 OR 3 AFFIRMATIONS TO START THE DAY:

_____

_____

_____

_____

WHAT IS YOUR TOP 3 PRIORITIES FOR TODAY?

_____

_____

_____

_____

EVENING:

WHAT GOOD DEED HAVE YOU COMPLETED THIS WEEK WHEN NO ONE WAS AWARE?

_____

_____

_____

_____

HAS ANYONE SHOWN UP FOR YOU THIS WEEK IN AN UNEXPECTED WAY?

_____

_____

_____

_____

DAY 6

CHAPTER REFLECTION BONUS

FOOD FOR THOUGHT

15 Day Challenge Journal Reflection Tracking

MORNING:

WRITE DOWN 2 OR 3 AFFIRMATIONS TO START THE DAY:

_____

_____

_____

_____

WHAT IS YOUR TOP 3 PRIORITIES FOR TODAY?

_____

_____

_____

_____

EVENING:

WHAT IS ONE THING YOU WOULD LIKE TO CUT OUT OF YOUR HABITS?

_____

_____

_____

_____

LIST WHAT WOULD MAKE CUTTING THE SELECTED HABIT EASIER:

_____

_____

_____

_____

DAY 7

CHAPTER REFLECTION BONUS

FOOD FOR THOUGHT

15 Day Challenge Journal Reflection Tracking

MORNING:

WRITE DOWN 2 OR 3 AFFIRMATIONS TO START THE DAY:

_____

_____

_____

_____

WHAT IS YOUR TOP 3 PRIORITIES FOR TODAY?

_____

_____

_____

_____

EVENING:

REFLECT ON ONE NEW THING OR EXPERIENCE YOU WANT TO TRY:

_____

_____

_____

_____

ARE THERE ANY BARRIERS TO MAKING THIS HAPPEN?

_____

_____

_____

_____

DAY 8

CHAPTER REFLECTION BONUS

FOOD FOR THOUGHT

15 Day Challenge Journal Reflection Tracking

MORNING:

WRITE DOWN 2 OR 3 AFFIRMATIONS TO START THE DAY:

_____

_____

_____

_____

WHAT IS YOUR TOP 3 PRIORITIES FOR TODAY?

_____

_____

_____

_____

EVENING:

TOP 3 PLACES YOU HAVE TRAVELED (CAN BE LOCAL)

_____

_____

_____

_____

TOP 3 PLACES YOU WANT TO VISIT:

_____

_____

_____

_____

DAY 9

CHAPTER REFLECTION BONUS

FOOD FOR THOUGHT

15 Day Challenge Journal Reflection Tracking

MORNING:

WRITE DOWN 2 OR 3 AFFIRMATIONS TO START THE DAY:

_____

_____

_____

_____

WHAT IS YOUR TOP 3 PRIORITIES FOR TODAY?

_____

_____

_____

_____

EVENING:

WHAT DO THINK IS YOUR BEST CHARACTERISTIC?

_____

_____

_____

_____

WHAT WOULD THOSE CLOSEST TO YOU SAY YOUR BEST CHARACTERISTIC IS?

_____

_____

_____

_____

DAY 10

CHAPTER REFLECTION BONUS

FOOD FOR THOUGHT

15 Day Challenge Journal Reflection Tracking

MORNING:

WRITE DOWN 2 OR 3 AFFIRMATIONS TO START THE DAY:

_____

_____

_____

_____

WHAT IS YOUR TOP 3 PRIORITIES FOR TODAY?

_____

_____

_____

_____

EVENING:

CLOSE YOUR EYES AND PRACTICE DEEP BREATHING FOR 10 MINUTES: (RECORD TIME COMPLETED)

_____

_____

_____

_____

ANY CHALLENGES WITH STAYING IN THE MOMENT FOR DEEP BREATHING EXERCISE?

_____

_____

_____

_____

DAY 11

CHAPTER REFLECTION BONUS

FOOD FOR THOUGHT

15 Day Challenge Journal Reflection Tracking

MORNING:

WRITE DOWN 2 OR 3 AFFIRMATIONS TO START THE DAY:

_____

_____

_____

_____

WHAT IS YOUR TOP 3 <u>PRIORITIES</u> FOR TODAY?

_____

_____

_____

_____

EVENING:

WHAT ARE A COUPLE WAYS THAT YOU SELF-CARE?

_____

_____

_____

_____

**WHAT IS A SELF-CARE ACTION THAT YOU LONG
FOR, BUT HAVE NOT EXPERIENCED?**

_____

_____

_____

_____

DAY 12

CHAPTER REFLECTION BONUS

FOOD FOR THOUGHT

15 Day Challenge Journal Reflection Tracking

MORNING:

WRITE DOWN 2 OR 3 AFFIRMATIONS TO START THE DAY:

_____

_____

_____

_____

WHAT IS YOUR TOP 3 PRIORITIES FOR TODAY?

_____

_____

_____

_____

EVENING:

WHAT ARE 3 THINGS THAT MAKE YOU FEEL COZY AND AT PEACE?

_____

_____

_____

_____

LIST ONE POSITIVE CHANGE YOU HAVE MADE THIS YEAR:

_____

_____

_____

_____

DAY 13

CHAPTER REFLECTION BONUS

FOOD FOR THOUGHT

15 Day Challenge Journal Reflection Tracking

MORNING:

WRITE DOWN 2 OR 3 AFFIRMATIONS TO START THE DAY:

_____

_____

_____

_____

WHAT IS YOUR TOP 3 <u>PRIORITIES </u>FOR TODAY?

_____

_____

_____

_____

EVENING:

WHAT IS YOUR LOVE LANGUAGE?

_____

_____

_____

_____

DO YOU BELIEVE IN SPIRIT ANIMALS? IF SO WHICH ONE, DO YOU SEE YOURSELF AS?

_____

_____

_____

_____

DAY 14

CHAPTER REFLECTION BONUS

FOOD FOR THOUGHT

15 Day Challenge Journal Reflection Tracking

MORNING:

WRITE DOWN 2 OR 3 AFFIRMATIONS TO START THE DAY:

_____

_____

_____

_____

WHAT IS YOUR TOP 3 PRIORITIES FOR TODAY?

_____

_____

_____

_____

EVENING:

WHAT WAS YOUR DREAM JOB AS A CHILD?

_____

_____

_____

_____

WHAT IS YOUR DREAM JOB OR BUISNESS TODAY?

_____

_____

_____

_____

DAY 15

CHAPTER REFLECTION BONUS

FOOD FOR THOUGHT

15 Day Challenge Journal Reflection Tracking

MORNING:

WRITE DOWN 2 OR 3 AFFIRMATIONS TO START THE DAY:

_____

_____

_____

_____

WHAT IS YOUR TOP 3 PRIORITIES FOR TODAY?

_____

_____

_____

_____

EVENING:

DID YOU ACCOMPLISH YOUR SHORT-TERM GOAL FROM DAY 2 EVENING PROMPT?

_____

_____

_____

_____

WERE THERE ANY CHALLENGES IN COMPLETING THIS? IF COMPLETED, EXPRESS WHAT YOU FEEL ABOUT THE ACCOMPLISHMENT:

_____

_____

_____

_____

Reflection Closing Message

It seems you've reached **DAY 15**. Amazing efforts on doing the work!

If you DNF (did not finish) that is absolutely okay too. The great thing about self-reflection, is you only need to apply the pace of yourself.

Whether you have the paperback version; or the e-book and was able to write notes separately. I hope that you are able to go back through the journey of the poetry, illustrations and reflective journeys again and again.

Inner work and processing can be hard. You're worth it; an empty jug can't pour into awaiting cups. Sometimes all you can do is live in the now and start at Day 1. Please spread the word to others you think may enjoy or benefit from this book. Feel free to message me your testimonials and connect with me. Turn to the next page for a thank you note and connecting information.

Thank You Note

I would like to take a moment and thank you for taking the time to journey through the pages of my book. Your openness to submerge your mind into my art means the world to me; even if just for a little while. It's my hope that you found something meaningful that resonates with these chapters. That ignite you to revisit the pages again and again.

With deep gratitude,

Thank you!

Please take a brief moment to rate and or review this book on amazon, good reads or whichever platform you're obtained this copy from. Whether short or lengthy I would like to hear from you. This also helps other readers when exploring for different selections of books to read. Consider leaving a review today, every review counts.

Let's Connect!

Instagram	Facebook	Amazon	Goodreads

Other Works By Q.M Gatlin

- o My Brain, My Way -A Creative Space for Personal Growth, Emotional Regulation and Mindful Living.
- o Crowned In Color- Coloring Book Journey
- o Shades of Desire (A Dark Romance) – Coloring Book Journey

When I am not writing or working; I like to take coffee breaks. If you would like to contribute to my coffee love fund. You can purchase me a coffee here:
https://buymeacoffee.com/qmgatlin

Coffee

.

www.ingramcontent.com/pod-product-compliance
Lightning Source LLC
Chambersburg PA
CBHW071325130626
46556CB00004B/1743